BLESSINGS AND CURSES

BLESSINGS AND CURSES

poems

Anne Whitehouse

POETIC MATRIX PRESS

PERSONAL ACKNOWLEDGMENTS

I would like to thank Julie Meslin for her close readings and suggestions for some of the poems and Paul Jessen for his advice about their organization.

Excerpt from "That Morning" from SELECTED POEMS 1957-1994 by Ted Hughes. Copyright © 2002 by The Estate of Ted Hughes. Reprinted by permission of Farrar, Straus and Giroux, LLC.

Cover Design by Ginger Nagy

Copyright © 2009 by Anne Whitehouse

ISBN: 978-0-9824276-3-7

All rights reserved. No part of this book may be used or reproduced in any manner whatsoever without written permission, except in the case of quotes for personal use and brief quotations embodied in critical articles or reviews.

Poetic Matrix Press
www.poeticmatrix.com

Acknowledgments

These poems in BLESSINGS AND CURSES have appeared in the following publications: Links to publications are available at www.annewhitehouse.com.

2River, Issue 12, no.1, Fall 2007
    CURSE VIII ("A collision in the park ...")
    CURSE XXIV ("Oh, for the potent substance...")
Adagio Verse Quarterly, Winter 2007
    CURSE III ("Sometimes tragedy can strike...")
    CURSE V ("You are going to get older...")
Brave Little Poem of the Day, June 21-24, 2007
    CURSE IV ("Someone overturned...")
Brave Little Poem of the Day, August, 2007
    BLESSING XXII ("Gretchen is the angel...")
Confrontation: November, 2007.
    BLESSING XXV ("When I was writing *Rosalind's Ring,*...")
Earth's Daughters: vol72 *Splinters and Fragments,* Winter, 2008
    CURSE XXII ("On September 1, 1939...")
Gander Press Review, 2009
    BLESSING IV ("Perennial blossoms...")
    BLESSING XXIV ("The redwood trees stand...")
The Golden Lantern, 2009
    A BLESSING AND A CURSE
The Oklahoma Review, Vol. 8, Issue 1, Spring 2007
    CURSE II ("My cousin's cousin...")
    BLESSING IX ("The magical rocks of Hamilton Falls...")
Phantasmagoria, Spring/Summer 2007
    BLESSING XXXVI ("I walked out on the beach...")
Saranac Review, Issue 3, 2008
    CURSE XV ("When Jeff's cell phone rings...")

Sixers Review, Spring 2009
    Curse IX ("He was not good or kind,...")
    Blessing XVI ("There is something to be said...")

Southern Hum, Vol II, Fall 2006
    Curse I ("Anxiety is my greatest curse...")
    Curse VII ("Now in her eighties...")
    Curse XVI ("Money's a sore subject for Lydia...")
    Curse XVII ("'In the apartment we shared...")
    Blessing III ("Some of my happiest hours...")
    Blessing V ("To my mind...")
    Blessing VI ("Jimi Hendrix's...)
    Blessing XXVII ("The student leaders at the University of Alabama...")

Southern Hum, Vol 2, issue 4, Summer 2007
    Curse IV ("Someone overturned...")
    Curse VI ("To be easily intimidated...")
    Curse XIX ("I lost a singular friend...")
    Curse XX ("Abby runs on a treadmill every morning...")
    Blessing XIV ("The island sparkles in the sun...")
    Blessing XIX ("In my dream I was standing...")
    Blessing XXXII ("An enchanted summer evening...")
    Blessing XXXVIII ("In science, elegance...")

The Dead Mule School of Southern Literature, Winter 2009
    Blessing XX ("One of the last sunsets of the year...")

*For Stephen and Claire,
my greatest Blessings*

Blessings and Curses

BLESSINGS AND CURSES

At the end of the Torah,
God appears to Moses
and tells him his life is over.
He will see the Promised Land
but not set foot in it.
Like his brother Aaron before him,
he will ascend the mountain and die,
but first he must address his people one last time.

Moses says to his people,
It is up to you to obey God's commandments.
This is more important to God
than ritual acts of sacrifice.
You must look into your hearts
and choose the words from your mouths.

Through Moses, God speaks directly,
"I call heaven and earth
to witness against you this day
that I have set before you life and death,
the blessing and the curse;
therefore choose life, that you may live,
you and your seed."

Afterwards, God returns
when Moses is alone.
He predicts, after Moses is dead,
His people will betray Him.
They will turn to false gods,
and He will punish them.
God asks Moses to compose a song
to remind the people of their obligations,

which Moses does instantly
and sings it to them,
enumerating God's blessings and curses.

Moses is as mysterious
in death as in life.
He died on Mount Nebo,
at the summit of Pisgah,
and was buried below
on the steppes of Moab,
but no one knows his grave.
The Torah tells us, absolutely,
Moses is the greatest leader
the Jewish people ever had.
Not since Moses has God
appeared face-to-face to any human being.

When Moses died, he left us
with God's blessings and curses
falling on us equally.
This is the life we are given.

Curse I

Anxiety is my greatest curse—
the worry I have offended someone,
forgotten an obligation,
missed a deadline, or slipped up
in one of seemingly endless ways
causes me panic and misery.

I pledge not to live in error,
perceiving myself powerless,
frustration blossoming to anger—
an ugly bloom, like a boil or a sore—
followed by regret,

ricocheting thoughts accuse
and attack me without relief.

Blessing I

Yanina never wears
rubber gloves
when she cleans
yet the skin on her hands
is as soft as a baby's
as if it were impervious
to the detergents and cleansers
it's in contact with.

To brush her palm
is to touch a flower petal;
her fingertips are
tiny cushions.

Blessing II

Bart bought Karen two dresses
at Barney's—one red, one blue.
She accepted his gifts
with grace and pleasure,
not plagued as I might be
by the fear that she
didn't deserve them
and so must reject them.

The only color she refused
to wear was solid black,
which distinguished her
in Manhattan.

One day stylishly
adorned in red,
another day, blue,
she related the story
about the dresses
she'd already told me—

reminding herself
what she's in danger of forgetting.

Curse II

My cousin's cousin
who pinned me in the kitchen
and groped my breasts
at Thanksgiving
is an ob-gyn in Texas
who refuses to counsel women
with unwanted pregnancies
on abortion.

His wife killed a coral snake
with a shotgun at their ranch.
It was curled up
on the front porch.
"I respect snakes,
but these kill the dogs."
She'd called her husband at work
and he'd declined to come home.

"Handle it yourself," he said,
and she did.
She got it with one shot;
the recoil nearly knocked her down.
Not wanting to scare her daughter,
she hid the evidence from her.

BLESSING *III*

Some of my happiest hours
have been my pink-and-gold dawns
beachcombing for shells on Sanibel.

Looking down, I tread lightly,
trying not to crush a single shell
searching among the spoils of nature
for the delicate, defectless ones
I never tire of finding—

treasures stranded
on sands soft as flour
deliciously cold and ridged
to my bare feet.

My husband said,
"You think they are valuable,
but they are worth nothing.
I like finding them, too.
Then I put them in a closet
and never look at them."

Yet he loves them
as a family heritage,
his grandparents' beloved activity
shared with their descendants,
which he's passed on,
unexamined, like the Unconscious,
influencing his idea of himself,
knowing and naming Nature.

As for me, I never tire of looking,
I feast my eyes
and see them change
in my perception.
Collected and sorted
in the drawers of my cabinet,
a thousand miles
from the sea of their birth,
they seem more beautiful
to me than works of art,
mysteries without
the animals that made them.

Curse III

Sometimes tragedy can strike
out of nowhere.
Everyday obligations pale
to insignificance
in the great shock;
ordinary life is put on pause,
and another life takes over.

When Patty's twenty-year-old son
was arrested at his college
and accused of selling a drug,
he was instantly expelled
and sent off to county jail.
There was nothing to do
but be afraid of the other men
in the cell. All day all
he got to eat were
cereal, two hot dogs,
and a dry ham sandwich.

Patty, Patty's husband,
and her son's father
had to find him a lawyer,
attend a hearing, raise bail,
endure the pressures
of having to react
to the awful power of the law
crushing down on their son,
while trying to rescue
his future for him,
and still mad at him

for letting this happen
to all of them.

"It's because he has red hair,"
said his mother.
"He stood out; the kids at school
made fun of him;
he couldn't find a girlfriend."

She dwelled on the past
as if it could make the present
make sense.

"Maybe he's being framed.
What he's accused of
was months ago.
I emptied his room at school;
it was absolutely clean."
She lamented,
"He's always trying
to help someone.
He has to learn;
he can't save the world."

Blessing IV

Perennial blossoms
in spring—
so delicate,
ethereal,
emerged from
chthonic earth
briefly,
once more,
to delight.

BLESSING V

To my mind
the greatest treasures
the Europeans found
in the New World
were not gold, silver,
copper, or precious stones,
wonderful as they are,
but the native foods
they married to their own cuisines.

Riches of my beloved
Hemisphere, I celebrate you;
you are native to me, too.
I have grown and thrived on you.
You have satisfied my hunger,
given me energy and health,
awakened in me
longings for your melded flavors.
I crave, and I eat,
and you satiate me.

At the basis of the diet,
the "three sisters"—
corn, beans, squash—
dried or ground into meal,
roasted or boiled,
made into soups or stews:
the seeds, kernels, and beans
spill out of the cornucopia,
millions and millions adding up.

Starchy, substantial
yams and potatoes,
luscious tomatoes,
varieties of peppers
for spice and fire,
who doesn't go a day
without one of them,
but loves above all
the divine dark
brown bitter nibs
of *theobroma cacao*—
drink of the gods.

One snowy January
Sunday morning
after the museum,
I stopped at Fauchon's
on Madison Avenue.
A boy and his father
sat next to me at the bar.
We ordered two hot chocolates;
in the thermos was not
enough for one cup,
which the bartender
split between us.
"It's not prepared here.
Each morning we get
three full thermoses
a lady makes for us
from her special recipe.

We're at the end of it now;
I'll let you have what's left."

He handed me and the boy
large delicate cups
of thin white bone china
each a third full of a liquid
so thick and luxurious
it was the essence of chocolate.
The wonderful aroma
crept up our nostrils;
we each spooned a drop
on our tongues,
tasting in silence,
while the bartender waited
with the boy's father.
Speechless, we tasted again;
it was as if we were dissolved
in this substance we ingested;
it had to be savored drop by drop;
if we tried to gulp it down
we would choke on it,
but just a small amount,
and we were rejuvenated.

We eyed ourselves
in the opposite mirror.
The boy looked at me
and spoke for us both.
"I feel so chocolate-y,"
he announced definitively.

Curse IV

Someone overturned
the pigeon's nest,
dropping out the eggs
onto the fire escape.
They smashed
against the iron landing,
instantly killing
the half-formed creatures
among the yolk and albumen
and broken bits of shell.

I'd seen the mating
atop an air conditioner—
how they twisted
their iridescent necks
around each other
in passionate embrace.
The feathers shone
emerald green, soft
fuchsia – how beautiful,
I thought, and saw
how he mounted her.
I felt privileged
to see it and carry
the memory away.

Last year,
of their three eggs,
one rolled out
of the nest,
one was rotten,
and one hatched.

I remember it
right after birth
so pitiful and scraggly,
it seemed unlikely
to survive,
but it grew fast
and in one day
learned to fly.
From the first,
awkward efforts
I wondered if
it'd make it;
it was gone
the next day.

But this year
there are no
more eggs,
no chicks
or fledgling
to leave the nest.
Those who despise
pigeons
will despise me
for writing this:
their life
is as worthy
as any other.

Blessing VI

Jimi Hendrix's
younger brother Leon
put it like this:
"I was laying in bed
and a purple flame
came out of the sky
and set the whole room
buzzing:
the flame knocked
the dust off the strings
of an old guitar
resting in the corner
that a lady had traded me
for some dope.

"My whole body was shaking;
I reached over
and grabbed it:
I could hear Jimi's voice
in my ear;
he was saying,
'Come on, baby brother,
you're ready.'
Ever since then
I been playing
like a man possessed."

Leon looks like Jimi
if Jimi had lived to be 56;
he has Jimi's manner
and dresses like Jimi
and plays a Fender Stratocaster

plugged into stacks
of Marshall amps,
but when he plays
(not left-handed),
he is definitely not Jimi
and never will be.

"Sometimes I say,
Have I lost my mind?
How could I dare play
guitar after Jimi?
Plus, I always
considered it a sacrilege.

"After our mother died
when we were children,
our dad was gone a lot
and Jimi looked after me.
He was my big brother,
best friend, surrogate dad.
He fed me,
took me to school,
taught me sports,
but he never
taught me guitar.
I fell asleep listening
to him practicing.
I tagged along to
band rehearsals,
gigs, and later on tour.

"Sometimes, when
I'm playing,
I'll ask him to help me.
I'll say, 'What'll I do now?'
and he'll say,
'Reach for it.'

I'm just scraping by.
All I got is a guitar
and six strings.
The other day
a collector wanted to buy
my blue one,
but I had to tell him
it's in the pawn shop now.
Hey, Jimi did it, too."

Curse V

You are going to get older;
there is nothing you can do about it.
Your bloom will fade,
your skin wrinkle.
Inevitably,
your body will fail you,
and one day
you will leave it behind.

This is the subject
of poets the world over
from the beginning of time.
There is no new thought
I can offer,
everything has
already been said.
I add my voice
to the chorus.

Prepare for the future
however you can,
try to find something
to enjoy every day,
even if it's only a song—
a song can take you far
into the reaches
of yourself.

Blessing VII

In the middle of last May,
after three successive rains softened the soil,
magicicada septendecim began to emerge
in great numbers from the earth.
For seventeen years it had lived underground,
feeding on the fluids of tree roots,
growing from ant-sized to wasp-sized.

The exodus began at sunset:
in perfect synchroneity the nymphs
appeared from tunnels underground
climbing whatever they could find,
trees or shrubs or telephone poles,
discarding dried-out carcasses
in the final molt to adulthood.

Soft and white at first,
as their exoskeleton hardened,
they turned dark and brittle
with lacy, orange-veined transparent wings,
orange legs, and beady red eyes.

In choruses in the sunlit treetops,
the males courted the females
with music made by ridged tymbals
vibrating against their abdomens,
the reverberating sounds arousing to both sexes.

The males played one song to locate females
and another to approach them with;
the females signaled their receptivity
in rhythmic wing flicks

increasing in speed and intensity,
while the males vied with each other,
each hoping to sing a duet
with a flickering female.

In the ecstasy of union her wings grew still
as he burst into the culminating solo.
In the Ohio River Valley,
at the height of the year,
they were as numerous
as drops of rain.
Large, clumsy fliers,
they frequently collided
with creatures and objects
moving or still.
Their shrill songs saturated
the atmosphere,
drowning the noises
of lawnmowers, traffic,
the roar of planes.

There was no harm to them,
no sting, or bite, or menace.
Their life was to sing, fly, mate, eat,
and bask in the light of day
and dark of night.
Birds and animals feasted on them.
They perished in droves,
their brittle corpses piled up
like leaves in autumn.

They were no plague but a blessing
to remind us of the vastness,
greatness, and mystery of creation.

They damaged only the tips of trees
where females lay their eggs,
which recovered after two months
when the eggs hatched
and the nymphs dropped to the ground
and dug tunnels in the earth
to aerate the soil and drain it,
there to develop in the darkness
of the next seventeen years.

Blessing VIII

Drawn to the desert solitude before dawn,
she walks in the moonlight and the starlight,
listening to the mysterious rustle of the wind
in the Chamisa bushes. At dawn,
even the dust on the ground shines white
in the heart of the old capital.
Bits of straw gleam in adobe walls.

Blessed by marriage,
she lets her husband and child sleep
while she drinks deep draughts
from the delicious well of solitude,
alive to birds and insects
and small animals in the brush,
the sun just coming up
and the wind blowing over like a wave.

In the peace and joy of these walks
she creates the voice within her
to send pure and strong and true
to the last rows of the theater.

In the shadows
the coolness survives
in the hottest part
of the summer day,
when even the lizards
wriggle out of the sun.

Her voice is like the scent of roses,
intense and evanescent.
Her gestures rapidly shape the air.

Energy pulses in the red heart of pain,
the white heart of longing,
yellow for acceptance,
lavender, pink, and rose.
The roses are blooming
in great abundance.

Curse VI

To be easily intimidated
is a curse.
When I was younger
I let other people
influence my behavior
against my will.
It is painful to think of now.
When I took their advice
against my better instincts,
I came to grief in my heart.

Sometimes a stranger
reached out to help me.
When I entered the Writing Division,
my father urged me to study Accounting
so I could support myself.
I went to one class—what a bore!
"You might as well
be in Business School,"
said my advisor, a poet.
I knew he was right
yet needed him to tell me
to drop the class.

With my mother, it was harder.
Today, failure is complete,
yet I am not to blame.
Still struggling with blame,
I hold this paradox in my heart.
After all these years
only my heart has changed.

Blessing IX

The magical rocks of Hamilton Falls
shine silvery even when dry
because of the mica.
Also mineral-laden schists,
they are not like New York City rocks
cropping up in big slabs,
but small pebbles tumbled
smooth and flat as coins
in the cold rushing waters
of Cobb Brook.

In the heart of summer
in the cleft of the forest
I submerge in the pools
at the top of the falls
and the bottom.

The pebbles lie still and gleaming
through the mantle of clear water
on the rocky, sandy bottom
where I touch down,
am released, rejuvenated.
Later, dried and dressed,
my feet in socks and sneakers
hiking back on the trail,
I can still feel the cold
tingling in my soles,
enlivening my being.

Blessing X

I am keeping silent,
spending the summer day
in solitude in the country.
Listening to the birds call,
I recognize only a few.
How have I lived so long
without learning to name them?

I touch a porch column
and am caught in a spider's web.
Last night, in the porch light,
I watched one casting
such a vivid shadow
against the house I thought
I was seeing double.
I couldn't spot the web at night,
but I watched the dance that made it,
the spider flinging itself across space,
catching itself on a thread,
spinning out more,
its forelegs knitting rapidly
as it braced itself for the next leap.

At the top point of the barn roof,
the wasps have built a nest.
I watch them fly in and out.

**

I am thinking of Eleanor
who lived here twenty-eight years,
first with Mark, then without him.
When she was alive,

piano music issued from this house
for several hours every day,
louder in summer
when the windows were flung open,
but also in winter,
muffled by panes of glass,
sinking soft as lamplight
on the snow.

A house with music is a blessing.
For Eleanor, cursed by deafness,
music came to live inside her.
Through a great effort of will,
she listened with her fingers.
How she did it I do not know,
but I watched her succeed
at the end of her long, blessed life.
Her love of the art
and the instrument,
the pleasure she took
in its difficulty and mastery
kept her at it day after day.
She surrounded herself
with images of angels.
Her abiding wish
was to instruct by delight.

Curse VII

Now in her eighties,
Erika sits in a chair in a circle of chairs
to tell us her story for *Yom HaShoah*.
"During the Second World War,
the British took in ten thousand children
from Germany, Austria, and Czechoslovakia.
I was one of them, sixteen years old in 1938.

"I was scared, lonely, unhappy.
When the *blitzkrieg* started,
the bombs fell indiscriminately all over London.
Then I felt better;
I had wanted to be like everyone else,
and now I was.

"I never dreamed my parents were murdered.
I didn't learn until after the war.
I was completely unprepared.
The way I felt—it's more than anger,
it's the deepest despair.
I lost my faith in God.
I'd made a bargain—
I'll get through all this,
and You'll reunite my family.

"The bargain was one-sided.
When I found out,
it was Yom Kippur, 1945.
I went to a non-kosher restaurant.
The meal I ate stuck in my throat,
but I wanted to make my point.

"After Chamberlain and Munich,
I remember my father saying,
'It's a good thing there's no war.
If there's a war, they'll kill the Jews.'
My parents might have known
they were saying goodbye for good
at the dock in Hamburg in 1938.

"I was the youngest
and they considered me useless.
All my efforts were for them.
I wanted to show them what I'd accomplished.
In some ways I've never gotten over it.
I think of what they did for me."

Erika's daughter Kim says,
"My mother was P.T.A. President
and led the Girl Scout troop.
She never talked about herself,
but I knew she was different.
When a friend said,
'Your mom has an accent,'
I replied, 'She does?'
my voice rising in a question,
knowing and not knowing."

Blessing XI

It is a blessing
to come to the end
of a long work.
Today, July 26, 2005,
I wrote the last words
of my second novel.
On the hottest day of the year,
when it was a struggle
to walk down the street,
I sat at my desk typing
the words of my mind
onto the computer screen
and felt light as air.

Blessing XII

The Sixties people are growing old and dying,
the ones who were going to change the world.
Pete Seeger can no longer sing his own songs.
When he strikes the gong, it has a hollow sound.
"Sixty years," he cries, mourning the anniversary of
    Hiroshima.

When Rev. Kenjitsu Takagaki rings the gong, it is resonant.
"May this bell bring happiness and peace within ourselves,"
    sounds the gong—
"May the music of the bell transform violence into
    compassion and peace,"
    sounds the gong—
"May we all be free from suffering, hunger, and pain,"
    sounds the gong.

Blessing XIII

When inspiration comes, attend to it.
Drop everything else. Listen carefully.
You get one chance and one chance only.
To receive the blessing,
you must be prepared to receive it.
Let yourself be its instrument.
The intention and expression are up to you.

Curse VIII

A collision in the park
between two runners—
I didn't observe it but heard the cry
and turned and saw a man on his side
not moving on the pavement,
and a woman standing not close but nearby,
watching him without approaching.

Clutching his elbow,
he screamed at her to go away
while she refused,
her hands folded across her chest,
her back bent like a question mark.

Some people stopped
and some kept walking.
Suddenly he wailed like an animal in pain;
twisting on his back, he kicked the air,
writhing while he cursed her.
She remained where she was
not leaving or coming closer.

Two teenaged girls exchanged looks
and hurried past;
an older man stepped up
with a cellphone,
but there was an ambulance
parked on the Drive.

The fallen man let loose
one more scream
and spread his arms wide

while medics lifted him
on a stretcher and evacuated him.
Not until he was gone
did she walk away.

Blessing XIV

The island sparkles in the sun
in the last mornings of summer,
as if it has dipped back
into the dark blue sea
and been washed overnight.
The grass tastes of salt,
sunlight glitters on the leaves
of bushes and trees and vines,
and the sand and stones
and earth all are damp.

Long-limbed just lately,
our girl runs through the yard,
with her dreamy smile,
her busy mind,
alive to her unfolding self.

Two days and nights before,
the island was lashed by rain.
In darkness we awoke
to the downpour
and embraced for dear life.
The rain fell around us,
hiding the moon and stars
and battering our little house,
and we remembered
an afternoon
in Venice long ago,
when running for cover
from a sudden cloudburst,
we were surprised by a man
singing of love

as he stood under the awning
of a restaurant
in the streaming summer;
as we crossed the piazza,
he opened his arms
and smiling gazed
into our eyes,
as if dedicating
his song to us.

Blessing XV

At the end of summer
the evening sky
is lavender and gold,
the leaves are dark, dark green.
The greatest love is one
that demands no response
but gives fully and completely.
I think of Hellen,
who loved me
unconditionally,
a child whom
she took to her heart
and sustained
into middle age.

Blessing XVI

There is something to be said
for being a renter,
of watching over a place
without the obligation
to improve it.

The Native Americans
made it a practice
to leave little trace of themselves
on the landscape.

Few of us can bear
to travel so lightly.
Yet this is our condition:
to occupy this life,
knowing we will
be parted from it,
but not when.

At sunset my shadow stretches
over the sea as I ease myself in
for the last swim of summer.
For thirty years I've immersed
in the cold waters of this cove
and felt cradled by sea and sky.
In their ever-changing immensities
I sense the unpossessable sublime.

I sink my restless thoughts to silence
so I may cleave to my true purpose.

Tethered, words enter the mind
through the eye or the ear,
to make of themselves
the weightless structure
apprehended wholly or in part,
like a shape shifting in the mist,
reverberant as a song,
to be taken up or forgotten,
like spent desire, or sunlight
shining on water, a fading reflection.

Curse IX

He was not good or kind,
but he was memorable.
He was the Poet,
and we the disciples
each week seeking
the benefit of his insight
as we sat around the table
listening politely
while he free-associated,
his random thoughts
drifting into *aperçus*
delivered in a high-pitched
nasal voice, the ash
hanging off his cigarette
until it dropped by itself.

At the interview
for admission to the class
I was in awe of him.
"These are yours?" he asked,
indicating my Fogg Poems.
In suspense I assented.
"Not bad," he continued,
and paused. "But there are
so many of them."
He sighed, leafing
through the seven pages
as if they constituted a burden.
"You're in the class," he said,
handing them back to me.

Believing he must be right,
I let him influence me.
From that day on
I dared not add another poem,
though possibilities still
occurred to me,
I ignored my ideas
until they went away.
At the time I didn't know
he was writing his own series
of loosely-titled sonnets
hundreds of them
he would publish
in multiple versions
under two titles.

    **

As winter melted into spring,
his mind grew unhinged.
One afternoon in class,
hearing workmen
making a racket
in the room below us,
he flew into a rage
and shouted at them
through the ceiling,
banging his chair
on the floor in retaliation.

Another time I saw him
shuffling across Mass. Ave.
in bedroom slippers
looking lost and dazed.

At his poetry reading at *The Advocate*,
he could barely speak.
The week before his collapse
he put aside student work
and, ignoring us,
closed his eyes and intoned,
"A bracelet of hair about the bone."

"A bracelet of hair about the bone,"
he uttered the line again
and again, in a trance,
his voice growing fainter
until at last he grew silent.

We fled, leaving him
clutching his dead cigarette,
the ash scattered on the table,
staring into nothing.

Curse X

"Financier, 73, plunges
nine stories to his death,
an apparent suicide,"
read the front page headline.

He made enough money
to fill a bank,
was one of the greatest
financial minds
of his generation
and mentor to a new one.
He had a lovely, loving wife,
four devoted sons,
two loyal brothers,
and friends as close as brothers.

He built his fortune
quietly and honestly,
with respect for others.
He showed charity
in deeds small and great:
paid his secretary's mortgage,
sent his shoeshine boy to college,
endowed a scholarship fund,
helped children learn to read,
and built a concert hall.
He could do whatever he wanted,
and he wanted to die.
**

In *Melymbrosia*, her first novel,
composed in her twenties
and unpublished at her death,

Virginia Woolf wrote,
"Candour forced her
 to consider
the extreme horror
of feeling the water
give under her,
of losing her head,
splashing wildly,
sinking again
with every vein
smarting and bursting,
an enormous weight
sealing her mouth,
and pressing salt water
down her lungs
when she breathed."

   **

The energy and activity,
the capital growth
he generated,
and the profits he made
were despite
his dark *doppelgänger,*
the unrelenting depression,
that clung to his back
and wouldn't let up.
Eventually it smothered
reason, light, life, and love.

"He took his pain
into his own hands,
and it is over,"
mourned his brother.

Blessing XVII

Neither brother nor sister
knew what they were fighting about,
but they kept fighting.
A life-long enmity
was at the source—
just the two of them
were siblings enough
in the family.

Barbs introduced their exchanges.
Nothing between them
was straightforward.
He couldn't resist twisting
the meanings of his words.
She was quick to be hurt
and blame him for it—
even eager, he would say.
Always armored, they were unwilling
to forgive and move on.
When their mother died
five years after their father,
the discord was final,
all contact severed.
Nearly thirty years passed
without their seeing
each other or speaking,
until they came together
at a daughter's
daughter's *bat mitzvah*.

Following decades of silence
in which there'd been born
a new generation,
with the length of their years
nearing the span
of their parents' lives,
brother and sister approached,
urged on by their spouses,
and when at last they spoke,
sparks didn't fly,
and the room didn't blow up,
leaving one of them dead.
At least they were able
to say hello to each other
if not much else.

Curse XI

"It was a perfect summer day,"
recalled Tomiko,
"August 6, 1945,
not a cloud in the blue sky.
At 8:15 in the morning,
I was in the schoolyard
doing exercises with my class.
We heard a plane flying over
and recognized
the vroom-vroom-vroom
of a B-29;
I wasn't scared
because they were often used
for reconnaissance.
Suddenly I saw a flash
like the sun
going into the ocean
bright red
but high in the sky.
We heard the noise
and were afraid.
We went down on the ground
as we'd been taught to do.
We put our eyes in their sockets
and closed our ears
and opened our mouths
to relieve the pressure
in the body
that a bomb creates.

"I lost my entire family.
I was thirteen years old.
I alone survived.

"For many years now
I've lived in Poughkeepsie,
in upstate New York.
I taught Japanese
at Vassar College
until I retired.
I love it up there.
Even so—hearing a plane
flying over the Hudson River,
I flash back.

"Be glad when you see a plane
that trails only white vapor,
with no bomb to drop."

Blessing XVIII

On an October day warmer than spring,
the leaves just beginning to turn color,
I turn a corner and encounter
the cold edge of a gusting wind
with its foretaste of winter.

Perhaps I'll wonder forever
about those junctures in our lives
when chance and fate entwine
becoming, in some sense, the same.

As a graduate student at Columbia,
I answered an ad for a tutor
and found myself hired to educate
a fifteen-year-old in all the subjects,
like a nineteenth-century governess.

Tara was weary of going to school.
She wanted only to ride her horses.
Her mother proposed an experiment:
mornings at the barn in Connecticut
if she studied on her own with me.

I was at my most academic,
full of intellectual fervor and plans
to be a font of knowledge for my pupil.
In reality, a gauche provincial,
my brain crammed full of facts and theories,
I hadn't a clue how to use authority
or inspire my student to a course of study.

But I had fun selecting books with Josephine,
the two of us traveling to the store by subway
both by chance in green-and-white plaid dresses,
yet she twice as old as I and far more elegant.

Coming from an upbringing with no use for indulgences,
I loved her generosity and openness
as she agreed on all the books I wanted
and paid, eccentrically, with five-dollar bills.

She was the most astonishing woman
I'd ever known, totally at ease in the world,
a visionary patroness of the arts
equipped with ardor and self-discipline,
well-connected, well-cared for, and well-born.

These qualities I admired, but most of all
how she impulsively embraced her pregnant
housekeeper with such depth of maternal feeling
I felt simultaneously embarrassed and deprived—
at once what I longed for and feared.

In her beautiful home, with its *objets d'art*,
my opinions were sought, even encouraged.
And yet I failed to know my place:
deep in conversation I kept the taxi waiting
and goofed off with Tara when the lesson was over.

My tenure as tutor was predictably brief.
"Tara's decided to go back to school,"
said Josephine, handing me a sealed check.

Stunned by the amount, I thought to refuse.
Her assistant privately talked me out of it.

"Let her do this," advised Deirdre, my own age.
"She made a mistake and wants to apologize.
It's more money to you than it is to her.
She's paying you off; don't make it hard for her."

My pupil was nowhere to be seen when I
thanked Josephine and departed from her life,
easily disposed of, and forgotten,
still blessed by the impersonal glow
of her ease and warm maternal confidence.

Curse XII

One sister wants
what three sisters have.
Everything she says
to them is calculated;
even her unconscious behavior
is usurpation.
Influenced by jealousy,
tight as a drum,
careless and destructive,
she makes havoc
wherever she goes.

Her sisters resent her—
the two with husbands and children,
jobs and independent lives,
and the sad sister,
still living like a child
at home with their parents
at the age of fifty.

Using misery
to gain attention
is a tactic of the desperate.

The youngest child, a boy,
lives intimately with hate.
When grown up, he curses his parents
and threatens his sisters with harm.
At thirty he courts a woman
nearly old enough to be his mother
who's a lawyer like his father
and everything he tells her
about himself is a lie.

Curse XIII

The way it was bred in us was ugly—
four sisters and a brother
set against one another
by parents in fierce contention
for their own scarce resources.

With a legacy of struggle and distrust,
so much jealousy and so little love,
we practiced stealth tactics,
intent on undermining each other.

By fighting with each other,
we justified our parents' discord.
They denied the results
of what they'd encouraged.
Anger became our common language,
the only discourse we shared
after speech failed.

Exhilarating the competition
when entered into willingly
with agreed-on limits;
on us it was imposed—
a zero-sum game where for one to win,
another had to lose.

Even now, I sometimes feel
the old insecurity deviling me
to prove myself unnecessarily
to my appalled opponent.

Mentally back in the family snarl
without knowing it,
I bear down like a steamroller
leveling everything in my way
that hasn't already fled.

How can I not see it
before I'm left in an empty field
gleaning regret, while birds fly over,
finding nothing, crying,
too late, too late?

Blessing XIX

In my dream I was standing
in the courtyard of a villa
built on a hillside
in a tropical country.
The soil was the color of ochre.
From it grew variety
upon variety of trees and bushes
whose branches and leaves
seemed carved of metal,
gray trunks amid dark,
glittering greens and golds.

And here and there a red flower or white.
I could apprehend only the details,
not the mysterious whole.
I breathed in the scents of earth
and flowers, water and decay,
listening to the parrots in the trees,
the shrill insects.
The equatorial night fell suddenly,
and in the fragrant darkness
a woman seemed to float toward me
from across the courtyard.
I couldn't see her clearly,
only shadowed features,
round face, upturned nose,
small, sturdy, delicate.

She extended her hands to me
they shone so white
I took them both in mine.

Their touch impossibly soft
filled me with rapture
I wanted never to let go.

I wasn't sure who she was,
a woman from the present or past.
Her features were vaguely familiar.
Had I dreamed myself a visitor
into her life?

I was confused and afraid.
Had I sought this attachment?
I didn't know what it meant
but when I tried to deny it,
I felt I was killing something.
Opposed by my doubt, she vanished.
I woke empty-handed,
with a vision and memory
that wasn't really a memory,
longing for such a touch
to caress my mind and free my thought,
bringing into expression
the frail idea in danger of perishing,
the flight of the mind
that moves without movement
to the stillness that is not death,
from life to the fullness of life.

Curse XIV

Janie perched over her bowl,
dainty as in the old days,
but nothing tempted her any longer,
not even the lettuce she used to love
with a relish exceeding any other.

For awhile she continued her passionate pleas,
hearing the rustling of a plastic bag.
They were so loud and piercing and wonderful
it scarcely seemed possible
that she could produce them,
this just-over-one pound ball of fur,
so sleek and compact,
with the little black line
straight across her pink nose
and the vibrating whiskers
that gave her such an inquisitive quality.

Guests were astonished
when they heard her shrieking
at dinner time.
Sometimes even I mistook her
for a strange and marvelous
musical instrument
overheard from the outside,
before discovering
it was my own pet.

Her first cries were alarum bells;
she was the most timid creature,
afraid of nearly everything
but her mother and me.

She liked to perch
on my shoulder, looking behind me
as I walked around the apartment,
the only one of our household
to have actually been born here.

In the dark of a February morning
in 2002, I woke to discover her brand-new,
in the cage cuddled next to her mother,
with a full coat of black-and-white fur,
already licked clean.

She never grew very large or brave
and stayed with her mother,
a fluffy gray-and-white guinea pig,
until the end of her mother's days.

The vet discovered their tumors on the same visit.
Dora Hellen's was more advanced.
Nothing we could do could change anything.
The mass grew bigger and harder
than a pregnancy,
then softened in her body,
destroying her intestines.

When Dora Hellen lay dying,
Janie tried hard to revive her,
placing her head under hers
and trying to lift her up
even after life had fled her.
After that, Janie was always alone.
Seven months later, the family curse

was killing Janie, too.
In her last days she crouched in her cage
facing into the corner for hours
like her mother before her,
an image of suffering and endurance.
She no longer liked to be held
or cling to my shoulder.
She stank, not of excrement,
as her mother had, but of urine.
She could not contain it.
It was spreading through her body
and poisoning her.

One night early in November
I returned home from my seminar
to discover her final struggle had begun.
Her legs splayed behind her.
A moan escaped her, eerily human.

Almost a shadow, she lay on my leg
and her small body swelled against mine
with such a full breath
I thought life was returning.

But it was the end of life
flushing through her belly, her heart,
her lungs, leaving her corpse.

Blessing XX

One of the last sunsets of the year,
red and purple,
               the quiet lawn
uncovered by melting snow,
the trees standing tall.

What I want
for the rest of my life
to go on like this.

Blessing XXI

Every weekend Paul heads north
Like a homing pigeon
To his beloved Taconic Ridge,
The long valley where his house lies
Nestled between woods and stream,
His screened-in porch and garden,
His barn and wisteria arbor,
The pooled water of the wetlands
And the view from his own hill
Overlooking it all.

Blessing XXII

Gretchen is the angel
Of the Homelessness Prevention Program.
She rescues people and animals
And keeps them together.

For people whom other people have let down,
A pet's love is healing.
There's no need to equivocate,
To justify themselves,
Or apologize for shortcomings.

People who've experienced
The intense communication
Between pet and human
Don't need to be convinced
Of the worth of Gretchen's work.

Those who are old, sick, poor,
Down on their luck and losing their homes,
Along with them lose everything else—
Their worldly goods,
The place and things that define them,
The habits they've grown,
Their sense of sinking roots in the earth.

"You're the only one I've spoken to
Who's brought me hope,"
Said Joan to Gretchen,
Faced with losing her cat
After losing her lover to cancer,
Then her lover's apartment.
"I don't know how I'd go on
Without Babycakes."

Curse XV

When Jeff's cell phone rings,
it plays a bar of his father's canon
composed nearly sixty years ago
as an assignment in graduate school.

"Mr. Glynbourne,
my wife and I listened
to your composition,"
said Professor Jonas Pintchik.
"We think you have
a promising future."

"I had no future,"
judges Francis at eighty.
"A number in the class did.
I was dumbfounded
to be singled out."

Flashes of pride flicker
against hard-won humility.
Music, his passion still,
inflicts pleasure and pain.

When his son Mark played
his DVD slide show
celebrating his daughter
for a family audience of ten,
Francis was so offended
by the soundtrack
that he grabbed the remote
and pressed mute
without consideration

for anyone else,
outraged and furious
at having to endure
three pop songs
matched to pictures.

We watched in strained silence,
the joy bled from the pictures
as each one filled the screen
without accompaniment
while Francis still fumed,
tightly clutching the remote.
Awkwardly, Mark
tried to fill in the gap
with impromptu commentary.

Even unheard, the songs
continued to do their harm.

Blessing *XXIII*

When Aunt Mildred finished *Fall Love*,
she phoned me long-distance from Louisville.
Her voice trembled with excitement.
I thrilled to think my novel had caused it.

Meanwhile, Steve was calling me to the table,
where he and Claire sat waiting to eat.
The food was ready, and so was Aunt Mildred,
her response rising uncontrollably, like sap,

or like my own characters who didn't hold back
when in love, though they might be deluded.
I longed to hear what she thought,
but the sacred family dinner hour intervened.

Pressed again, I promised to call her back.
While I was eating, my thoughts wandered
to my literary great-aunt, with her interests
in Pamela Hansford Johnson and C.P. Snow,

her memberships in three book clubs,
her fondness for words and talk, gardens and travel,
her favorite city, London, where she'd rented a flat
and gone to Wimbledon every day.

What would *she* have to say about my confused,
hot-blooded, lonely artists, adrift in themselves,
seeking and not finding, self-indulgent
and self-abnegating at the same time?

My busy, useful aunt, with her droll expressions,
her sturdy chair for her aching back,

her expertise in math, her preferred drink
Scotch-and-milk in a bourbon town,

her messy house, and her modern art—
if, reading my book, this old, gray-haired lady
could lose her life in my characters,
all aglow with *their* ardors and agonies,

then I'd feel I'd done something. I thought
I'd heard in her voice the authentic note,
and as soon as I could, I called her back,
wanting to hear it again.

But it was not to be. Try as I might,
I couldn't elicit her first reaction a second time.
In its place, a sober, loyal assessment was taking shape.
And I never heard her sounding like a young girl again.

My hope was deferred to one of those afterlives
where only our imaginations take us,
where we rehearse to our satisfaction
what could have been, but was not.

Her lost response was intoxicating,
like that wildness that steals over our nerves
just when the snow is melting, and wetness
streams in slick rivulets down the black streets,

where the sun's reflection bobbles and dances,
and nothing is fixed or solid, but trembling
and thawing and flowing and changing—
like a bubble wavering in balance on the Great Divide.

Blessing XXIV

The redwood trees stand
like sentinels on the lonely coast,
the tips of their lofty spires lost in fog,
shaggy trunks and fragrant needles
dripping in the rain that swells
Redwood Creek as it tumbles
from Mt. Tamalpais to the sea.

"Saving these woods from axe & saw,
from money-changers and water-changers
is the most notable service to God & man
I've heard of since my forest wanderings began,"
wrote John Muir in gratitude to William Kent
after Kent bought the land to preserve it
in Muir's name with his blessing.
"If we lost all the money we have
and saved these trees, it would be
worthwhile," vowed Kent to his wife.

Such a racket echoed through Muir Woods
the day we saw that one salmon
struggling upstream, flapping half out of water.
The sound of it drowned out everything else.
All our lives we'd heard of its grueling
uphill journey at the end of life
yet until that day we'd never seen one
fighting the swift shallow current,
striking through the surface in great blows.
We waited on the bridge and watched it go
out of sight up the rocky-bottomed creek.

Curse XVI

Money's a sore subject for Lydia.
"I've been poor all my life,
And I guess I always will be."

Acting, writing, selling advertising—
She's tried them all and done them well.
She has beauty, charisma, and charm,

Yet finds herself in her early sixties
A part-time yoga instructor laid off
From her other job at a social diary

Website, unable to land other work,
Wrangling with Unemployment officials
To try to get thirty dollars a day.

The frustrations dealt her
Demand reserves of steely patience.
There is always one form lacking,

A new regulation called up to thwart her.
Her family lives far away. A roommate
helps pay the rent. Fifteen years ago,

She could have bought her apartment
At an insider price. All she lacked was
A down payment. Yet, she had saved

In reserve the precious family jewels,
Edna's pearls, given to her
Twenty-five years before by her mother-in-law.

How Lydia loved those pearls,
Large and lustrous, with a pink glow.
As if it were today, she could picture

Edna's queenly air as she had fastened the clasp
Around Lydia's neck and, stepping back,
Exclaimed how well they became her.

An actress herself, Lydia thought she'd divined
An undertone of regret in Edna's praise,
Which made her value the gift all the more.

Years passed. Lydia divorced, and Edna died.
The pearls were mostly locked up.
At last the time had come to cash them in.

She took the necklace to Christie's for an estimate.
As she untied the velvet wrappings for the appraiser,
She trembled, imagining lofty numbers

And felt close to buying her apartment.
It made her happy to think of it as hers—
The large, shabby, comfortable rooms

Where she'd lived so long and raised her son,
And all five kitties had room to roam,
Home to her primitive art, her shelves of books,

With high ceilings and wooden floors,
Closets and moldings, the views down Broadway.
Maybe one day, she wouldn't need a roommate.

These thoughts swirled in her brain while the appraiser
Peered at the pearls through a magnifying glass.
He picked them up and rolled them in his palm.

He seemed puzzled. "Well?" she asked.
"Don't you know? They're paste."
"No!" she cried. Yet, she had to believe it.

Bitter to think how she'd been fooled!
All this time she'd treasured a fake.
Now she couldn't buy the apartment.

Fast forward fifteen years. The apartment's
Increased in value manifold. She's glad
of her right to remain at a stabilized rent,
But her chance to make a fortune is gone.

Blessing XXV

While I was writing *Rosalind's Ring*,
there were times when I felt so afraid
before I could write I had to pray
to make a safe place without censure
where I could allow myself the freedom
to visualize what lay ahead for my characters.

I passed months and years in that pitch darkness
groping my way a fraction at a time,
getting lost sometimes for weeks,
having to go back and begin again.

For someone of greater gifts, perhaps,
it wouldn't have been so hard,
but this was my story, and mine alone,
only I had to discover it.

Now it is done and lies complete,
as if it had always existed,
and I'd had but to write down
what I'd known.
                  Go, Reader, to Your ease!
May You give minutes where I spent years!
The effort means nothing to the work,
but it is everything.

Blessing XXVI

The lovers were reunited after 42 years
in The Grolier Club catalog
and exhibition, *No Other Appetite*:
he almost impossibly handsome,
she, protean, with a different appearance
in every picture, intensely alive
and in thrall to death,
her imagination on fire,
and he drawn to magic, with a shaman's power,
skilled in productive trance,
the two doomed and blessed "to
go round the dark of the mind's moon
and come back to us as poetry."

Completing her part of the catalog,
curator Karen fell ill. "You have to be hardy
to take on Plath and Hughes."
When curator Stephen visited Hughes
at Court Green in 1996,
it felt familiar from Plath's descriptions
of the life they'd hoped to make there.
"Of course that all went bust," said Stephen,
"but there he is, I thought,
in the house they picked out together."

Book designer Bruce worked 12 days straight
till he was done. Driving home
in the White Mountains he saw
a pair of black bears off the road.
"It was a couple," Karen recalled he'd said,
as she recounted in her lecture,

"Soon after, I was driving near my house
in Easthampton. There in an orchard
I saw *my* two black bears, a couple also,
and the male looked at me right in the eye."

Then for a sign that we were where we were
Two gold bears came down and swam like men
Beside us. And dived like children.
And stood in deep water as on a throne
Eating pierced salmon off their talons.

So we found the end of our journey.

So we stood, alive in the river of light
Among the creatures of light, creatures of light.

Curse XVII

"In the apartment we shared,
Camille had her phone, and I had mine.
After she died, her parents called her number
sometimes fifty times a day just to hear
her voice on the answering machine.
I know why they did it;
I don't blame them.
But it was a small apartment,
and there was nowhere for me to go.

"On September 10, Camille had sat
around the table with me and Joshua.
She said she hated her job
and did it only to please her parents.
We got her to call them
and tell them the truth.
The next morning, I almost
said to her, 'Don't go to work.'
How many times since then
have I wished I did!

"A couple of weeks later,
I bombed the LSATs.
I got into just one law school, in L.A.
It was a way out, and I took it.
A fresh start, I thought.
                    What a mistake!
No one I knew in California
could understand what I was going through.
All the time I wanted to tell Camille about it.
She was my best friend.
"I went to class, I kept exercising.

I looked all right,
but inside I was crumbling.
I almost had to flunk out
before I could admit to myself
I needed to take time off.

"My parents didn't want me to.
They said, 'You'll never go back,'
but they were wrong.
Now I'm about to graduate,
not at the top of my class,
but at least I didn't fail.

"In the years after Camille died,
everything fell apart—
with my parents, my brothers,
with Joshua.
I'll never get over it,
but in a strange way,
she's become a part of me.
Sometimes that's what
keeps me going.
I think of her every day."

Blessing XXVII

The student leaders at the University of Alabama
organized peer brigades to rid the grounds
of rocks, bottles, soda cans, anything
that could be used as a weapon.
The campus was locked down,
guards posted at every entrance
to keep outsiders away.

No one dared admit to wanting integration.
The effective appeal was to pride.
"What will the country think of us?
We don't want to be another Mississippi."

In preliminary talks with student leaders,
James Hood had to be smuggled onto campus
huddled on the floor of the backseat of a car.

On June 11, 1963, personally escorted
by Deputy Attorney General Nicholas Katzenbach,
James Hood and Vivian Malone approached
Foster Auditorium to register for classes.
The governor stood in front and blocked their way.
 "Some people enter your life and leave it empty,"
said Hood. "Other people you never forget."

"Segregation now, segregation forever!"
declaimed Wallace for show.
National Guard General Henry Graham urged him
to step aside, and the two students entered, unhurt
and unhindered. Said Vivian, "I went beyond
that day in my mind to envision the future.

There will come a time in your life
when you must act for others. Everything
you have done until then is preparation."

Curse XVIII

It's Spring again, Lucie's favorite season—
cold, dewy, sunlit mornings,
pale blossoms against the sky.

The day before she died,
she was moved to a private room
with a view of Central Park.

It meant something to us
to point it out to her, even if
she didn't know what we said.

She fought for every breath.
Breathing was all she could do—
pure oxygen—her cheeks puffed up,

the mask half-covering her face,
her eyes like brown slits focused inward.
Her struggle was mortal and terrible.

It was hard to watch it,
hard not to wish it over.
She was drowning inside,

as she held the stuffed bunny
little Lucie had given her,
and Sonia stroked her brow.

Blessing XXVIII

Poets give their poems away
because they are written for joy.
A flash, a feeling concentrates;
a braided rope of meaning and sound
descends for me to climb,
and I feel the blessing radiate
through my being like sunlight.

Every day, all over the world,
documents are being issued,
examinations and licenses,
petitions and contracts,
declarations of war and peace,
diagnoses, analyses, prescriptions, laws—
words used to try to govern
our ungovernable instincts.

Thus employed, words
are negotiable, interchangeable.
But for poets, words
have weight and color and music.
The poet, watching and listening,
follows a mysterious impulse.

Curse XIX

I lost a singular friend,
Whose love of arcana
Made looking at paintings,
Sculpture, ceramics—
All fine or decorative arts—
Like going on a treasure hunt.

I had objected to her son
Pushing my daughter into the street.
She wasn't shoved with malice,
But with an enthusiasm
That overwhelmed her.

Just as I spoke, I regretted it
But was stubborn and kept on.
I was greeted with the click
Of the phone hanging up
And then silence forever.

I had crossed an unforgivable boundary.
At first I didn't believe it,
But she refused my calls,
And the reports came back,
"She doesn't want anything
To do with you."

I'd be the first to admit
She was a puzzle,
Rigid yet unpredictable,
She'd always tell a lie
Before the truth even when
There was no benefit.

It made no difference what I thought;
She'd given me up.

Four years passed—
A college span—when I saw her
In a stationery store at Christmas,
Accompanied by her son
And a friend's daughter.

I took the plunge and greeted her first,
But she never looked at me.
She talked for twenty minutes,
And everything she said
Was to my daughter.
What a desolate feeling
It gave me!

I sat brooding the next morning
When the phone rang.
A boy sounding vaguely familiar
Asked for my daughter.

"Who may I say is calling?"

There came silence,
Then muffled laughter.
I asked once more;
The indistinct reply
Sounded like "Gaby Ray."

My voice grew sharper,
"Who are you?"

I could hear a whisper,
Not to me, "What should I say?"

There was someone else
Not speaking into the phone.
I could barely hear it,
But I recognized her.

The boy said, not to me,
"I can't do this."
Then I was sure who he was
And who'd put him up to it.
Quietly, I hung up the phone
And this time knew it was final.

Blessing XXIX

Years ago I lived with a secret.
It fed me with such energy.
For a few, unforgettable moments,
I was swept away.

It was like an addiction.
I no longer knew what was real.
I gave to it more than was wise
And came to misery.

What was clear was no future.
I stopped believing in it.
One secret burrowed inside another,
Blanketed in forgiveness.

Curse XX

Abby runs on a treadmill every morning.
Her fast, steady pace consumes
Five miles in thirty-five minutes.
Some days, she finds it's more
Of a struggle than others,
But at the end, covered in sweat,
She always feels wonderful.
This is the gift she gives herself;
The rest of the day is Ben's.

Alan is less driven.
He has a bad leg and likes to swim
Or gently float in the pool
In a meditative state,
Cultivating patience and resolve.

Alan defers to Abby when it comes to Ben,
And Abby wants to keep Ben at home.
No one else will care for Ben as she will.
Ben doesn't like to be left alone.
He depends upon her for reassurance.

When Ben was eight months old,
They noticed he was different.
Six months later, the doctors
Gave them little hope:
"He's severely retarded
Physically and mentally;
He'll never have a normal life."

At eighteen Ben fixates on ideas.
"The man at the store," he says.
"Which man?" asks his parent.

"The man with the tie."
"You mean the man at the store
who was wearing a tie?"
"Yes. That man. At the store.
With the tie."
So the conversation goes,
Like running in place.

Alan says, "Sometimes I wonder
What it would be like
To go on vacation
Like a normal family.
Ben can't handle crowds of people,
Unfamiliar settings, airport security.
Except for short car trips,
We stay home.

"Now Ben goes to school
And day camp in the summer.
We have a wonderful babysitter
In whom we trust.
But soon Ben will be too old
For his school and camp.
There's a place fifty miles away from us,
A private institution.
It's expensive, but we could manage.
I asked Abby, 'Why don't we try it
A few days at a time, as a respite?'
But there were things about it
She didn't like, and she said no.
Abby may live forever,
But I know I won't."

Blessing XXX

The relief I felt when at last
The fly flew out the door!
It was a big fat black fly
That flew in through the torn screen
But couldn't fly out.

It buzzed incessantly for two days,
Zigzagging into walls,
Trapped inside the house.
I didn't want to kill it;
I wanted to free it.

In advance, I opened
Doors and windows for it,
And every time, perversely,
It flew away, landing somewhere else,
Buzzing endlessly.

It was louder than any fly
I'd ever heard.
It didn't know where to go,
But it wouldn't stop
Stupidly retracing its flight

Until at last it landed
On the back door as I was passing.
I opened the door, holding my breath,
And gently pushed it wider
Until the fly flew out forever

Leaving blessed quiet.
Finally at peace, I relaxed.

I repaired the screen.
At last, I thought,
I can finish writing my chapter.

Blessing XXXI

I write between the ticking of two clocks
made by Uncle Jack forty-seven years apart—
the mantel clock in the living room,
the wall clock in the foyer.

Their tick is comforting, human, imperfect.
They must be wound and regulated.
"Quartz movements are more accurate,
but they have no soul," he said.

Listening to his clocks scanning time,
I settle in the quiet, filtering out the world,
following the trail of an unheard voice—
it is myself, who only speaks to me.

Blessing XXXII

An enchanted summer evening,
fireflies glimmering
among colored paper lanterns,
music wafting in the beer garden—
the ironic lyrics and wistful melodies
of middle-aged men.
You say, "In some part of my mind
I'm always eighteen."

Once I fell in love
with the image of a boy
that I found in another boy.
It was nostalgia I was in love with,
the sudden opening
of the past into the present.

A water lily blooms
in the garden's fountain.
Past the warehouses and docks,
tankers and barges and great ships
pass in the deep channel
of dark and dirty water.

Blessing XXXIII

Two grasses, twisted together,
nourished by the same earth and sun,
buffeted by winds, soaked by rains,
bending down and springing back,
tossed in the warm, billowing air
or buried in snow, old and sere—

my husband, have you guessed
I am writing of us?

Curse XXI

To be left-handed is to be
Part of a permanent minority.
The world is always seeking
To trip us up.

In kindergarten
My scissors wouldn't cut.
It was the same with my daughter;
She "lagged in fine motor skills."

Every test I took in school,
I sat all twisted,
My left forearm reaching over
To rest on the right-sided desk.

Coffee makers, can openers,
Egg beaters, mixers, food processors—
All are designed to be operated
With the right hand.

Only in driving
Do we have the advantage:
Shifting with our right hand,
Steering with our left.

Why was this rule established
Here, and not in England?
I've often wondered,
Was a lefty involved?

Blessing XXXIV

"In one dream I was trapped
in a burning building
and couldn't get out.
Everyone had fled
and I was left behind.
In another dream
I was captured by aliens
and stranded in outer space.

"My dreams were attempts
to understand what
was happening to me.
All that first month
I was in a coma
I had only one good dream
that I remember.
There was a brass spigot
and water was pouring out of it—
cold, crisp, clean water.
I drank and drank.
It was so delicious
I wanted to keep on drinking.

"Then came a dream
where I was trapped in a car
and a man peered in
and said, 'I'm Clifford Wynne.
I used to work with your father.
Do you remember me?'

"'Sure, Mr. Wynne,' I said,
'I'm stuck in this car

and if you could give me
a hand and help me out,
I'd appreciate it.'
'I'll see about that,' he said.
'I'll get some help.'

"It turned out Clifford Wynne really
was there with me, in the ICU.
The next thing I remember
is my brother. He said,
'Hi, you're back,' and I said,
'Where have I been?'
He said, 'You've been
unconscious for a month.'

"I have no recollection
of the accident.
I could hardly believe it,
because I've been riding
motorcycles for thirty years,
but that's apparently
what happened:
the kid came right out
in front of me.
He said he didn't see me.
An SUV was behind me.
I'm lucky to be alive.
I'll never be what I was;
I'm someone different now."

Blessing XXXV

Slowly I'm achieving
a baby's perfect posture,
when it learns to sit
without any strain,
shoulder blades
pressing into the back
like folded wings,
the shoulders back, too,
the crown of the head
over the soft palate and throat,
in line with the heart
down to the pelvic floor,
seat of the body.

My body fills with breath,
my heart at front and center,
thoughts dissolved,
softening, deepening
into the interval
where a goddess passes by.

Curse XXII

"On September 1, 1939,
when war broke out,
I locked myself in the bathroom
and wouldn't come out.
I was crying; I knew
my world was ending.

"We had a good life in Warsaw.
My father owned a business;
we kept two servants;
my sister and I went to private schools.

"After one week the city was bombarded
from morning to night.
Warsaw was beautiful,
and it was completely destroyed.

"No one knew at first
of Hitler and Stalin's secret pact.
Soon the city was reorganized
and the ghetto set up.

"Young Jews were going to Russia.
Before the ghetto was closed,
my fiancé and I escaped
across the green border to the East.

"It wasn't so easy.
He was very smart at arranging things
and on the black market bought me
an original birth certificate

of a person my age
who'd been taken to Siberia.

"I spoke excellent Polish
because we'd spoken Polish at home.
He and I lived in the suburbs of a city
that was *Judenrein*.
I looked Jewish but he didn't.
He had blond hair and blue eyes.
"One day he left in the morning
and didn't come back.
I still don't know what happened to him.
The Germans picked him up.
They killed people for nothing.
With men, it was simple,
'Pull down your pants.'

"My parents perished
in the Warsaw Ghetto.
My sister died with her daughter
in a terrible concentration camp.
She couldn't think like a person
after her husband died
in the Army in the short war.

"He was wounded at the front
and brought to a hospital in Warsaw.
The Germans used poisoned bullets.
His wounds weren't mortal,
but infections developed.

"My second husband
saw his wife and daughter
killed before his eyes.
There are things you don't talk about
or understand.
Until the end of his life
he screamed in his sleep
and I would hold him.
He was a good husband,
a good father, a good man.

"For a year and a half,
until the end of the war,
I survived on my own without means,
with no family or home.
I had a twenty dollar bill
to buy my life if I were arrested.
No one knew I existed.
I believe I was fated to live;
I don't know why.

"Truman is my favorite president
because he let us in the U.S. after the war.
In New York I found my cousin.
She took me into her bedroom
and showed me her photo albums.
'Take what you want,' she said.
Can you imagine what it meant to me
to have a picture of my parents?"

Blessing XXXVI

I walked out on the beach,
and there it was, right in my path—
the rare Junonia,
most prized of Sanibel shells,
winking at me in the early morning.

Not a perfect specimen—
the tip gone,
some of the square
brown markings faded,
but of a decent size,
with whorls on the lip,
delicate and heavy
as if carved from stone,
on the inner curve
a lovely sheen.

I could scarcely believe it:
a shell I'd sought for thirty years
and never found was now mine.
It seemed it had come to me
without my looking for it.

So it is, I think, with so much
that we seek:
the thing will reveal itself
only in its time.

Blessing XXXVII

Once a friend interrupted me
while I was writing a poem.
I was deep in concentration

and the sound of his car startled me
as he pulled in the yard.
The car stopped, I saw him at the window.

I jumped up and met him at the door.
It was summer, it was raining.
I felt glowing and taller than usual.

Shyly, I told him what I was up to.
For once the poem didn't desert me.
In that blessed place, it came back.

Blessing XXXVIII

In science, elegance
is brevity;
the simplest
synthesis succeeds
best.

In art, elegance
is style—the pallor
of Madame X's
long neck and
sloping shoulders,
her melancholy profile.

The dark-eyed woman
was a life-long
philosopher,
happiest when
reading. Her hands
reached out to books
as if to love.

"My library
is an archive
of longings.
Art is what is true
whose reverse
is also true.
I was looking
for my life
to interpret
my dreams."

Curse XXIII

"In two months of sifting through the wreckage,
we found not one desk, or chair,
or Xerox machine, or computer.
They were two 110-story office buildings,
and they turned to dust.
The biggest piece of equipment I saw
was a piece of a telephone key pad
two inches square.

"I found the body of a woman
encased in rubble.
She looked pregnant.
We had a body bag ready
but were called from the site
as it was collapsing,
If only we had gotten her out,
her family could have had a decent funeral.

"We worked in 24-hour shifts.
As the days became weeks,
we accepted there wasn't anyone to find.
It was beyond discouraging;
it was hard to understand.
People cheered us
when we came off our shifts,
but we didn't feel like heroes.

"When those buildings fell
they took something from me
that I haven't gotten back.
The memories intrude
on my happiest moments.

At my daughter's high school graduation,
I found myself picturing it
without me there."

Blessing XXXIX

Shaking with fever,
Air passages clogged,
I kept falling in and out
Of a book I wasn't enjoying
But felt I had to finish
One way or another.

I used up a box of Kleenex
Staying up all night.
Time fell into a long warp.
I coughed until my ribs ached;
Cold and hot got confused.
In the morning I called the doctor.

Medicine was his art.
Touching my skin with a fingertip,
He told my temperature exactly.
Listening to the echoes
Of my voice through my lungs,
He located the infection.

The drug rapidly melding
Into me made me dizzy.
At last sleep overcame me,
Drenched in sweat
As the fever broke,
Like rain after a drought.

Blessing XL

On the first day of spring
that first breath full
of cold air and strong sun
exposed the newborn
as it passed from car to door
dangled in a car seat
held securely by Daddy.

The youngest child on the block
didn't open its eyes.
All the same
the breath of the world
stirred a changing expression
on its face.

Curse XXIV

Oh, for the potent substance
that could heal me from affliction!
Criticized, I brood and suffer.
I turn on myself
and eat out my heart.

From my window I watch
a tiny silver helicopter,
like an ornament or a toy,
heading south
in a blue-and-white sky.

Whirling gusts pluck
the last leaves from the trees.
My mind babbles;
I am plagued by thoughts.
How to extract the quiet self,

the one that doesn't speak,
but writes? Where fidelity
and honesty are one?
Say of me, I listened.
Say of me, I tried to understand.

Yet I made it harder than it had to be,
afraid of attention,
unwilling to permit mistakes.
When laughter could have helped,
I wouldn't let it.

Let these curses dry up,
light as leaves, and blow away.
The struggles are unending.
They are life itself.
They have my attention.

A Blessing and a Curse

One summer afternoon in the 1980s
when the air was fetid and muggy
and the city streets filthy and miserable,

I impulsively looked for refuge
in the American Museum of Natural History,
that storehouse of human knowledge

of what lies within our universe and ourselves,
with its millions of artifacts and specimens,
the accumulations of generations

of explorers among isolated peoples
and unpeopled regions, of the unrecorded past
collected, investigated, and placed into context.

**

I don't remember how I ended up in the room
where the Buddhist monks were making a Mandala
by pouring colored sands from little bottles

to form intricate patterns. They worked their designs
on a tray on a table in the middle of the room,
while viewers watched and cameras recorded their moves.

Three men with shaved heads in saffron robes:
one was older, and two were young. As soon
as I entered, I felt their peace and wanted to stay.

One of the younger monks explained
how the museum had invited them to New York
from their monastic exile in northern India.

They carried the images they made in their heads.
The Mandala would take two months to finish.
"And then?" I asked. He smiled, and his gold tooth

winked at me. "We will take the Mandala
to the Hudson River and offer it to the water.
The museum wants to preserve it.

They will use sprays to fix the sands,
but they won't work. It will be given back;
the cycle must continue."

I remember the lightness in his voice,
the rippling muscles of his lifted arms,
a grace that seemed without sex, outside of time.

I was older than he, though still apprentice
to my art. I thought of the beautiful designs

of the Wheel of Life, their inner meanings
and mysteries, and the interplay of colors.

It seemed tragic to me, but not to him.
His inner equilibrium wasn't disturbed.

It mattered not to him that nothing lasted,
and I counted it a blessing and a curse.

Contents

BLESSINGS AND CURSES ("At the end of the Torah...") 3
CURSE I ("Anxiety is my greatest curse...") 5
BLESSING I ("Yanina never wears...") 6
BLESSING II ("Bart bought Karen two dresses...") 7
CURSE II ("My cousin's cousin...") 8
BLESSING III ("Some of my happiest hours...") 9
CURSE III ("Sometimes tragedy can strike...") 11
BLESSING IV ("Perennial blossoms...") 13
BLESSING V ("To my mind...") 14
CURSE IV ("Someone overturned...") 17
BLESSING VI ("Jimi Hendrix's...") 19
CURSE V ("You are going to get older...") 22
BLESSING VII ("In the middle of last May...") 23
BLESSING VIII ("Drawn to the desert solitude before dawn...") 26
CURSE VI ("To be easily intimidated...") 28
BLESSING IX ("The magical rocks of Hamilton Falls...") 29
BLESSING X ("I am keeping silent...") 30
CURSE VII ("Now in her eighties...") 32
BLESSING XI ("It is a blessing...") 34
BLESSING XII ("The Sixties people are growing old and dying...") 35
BLESSING XIII ("When inspiration comes, attend to it...") 36
CURSE VIII ("A collision in the park...") 37
BLESSING XIV ("The island sparkles in the sun...") 39
BLESSING XV ("At the end of summer...") 41
BLESSING XVI ("There is something to be said...") 42

CURSE IX ("HE WAS NOT GOOD OR KIND...") 43
CURSE X ("'FINANCIER, 73, PLUNGES...") 47
BLESSING XVII ("NEITHER BROTHER NOR SISTER...") 50
CURSE XI ("IT WAS A PERFECT SUMMER DAY...") 52
BLESSING XVIII ("ON AN OCTOBER DAY WARMER THAN SPRING...") 54
CURSE XII ("ONE SISTER WANTS...") 57
CURSE XIII ("THE WAY IT WAS BRED IN US WAS UGLY...") 58
BLESSING XIX ("IN MY DREAM I WAS STANDING...") 60
CURSE XIV ("JANIE PERCHED OVER HER BOWL...") 62
BLESSING XX ("ONE OF THE LAST SUNSETS OF THE YEAR...") 65
BLESSING XXI ("EVERY WEEKEND PAUL HEADS NORTH...") 66
BLESSING XXII ("GRETCHEN IS THE ANGEL...") 67
CURSE XV ("WHEN JEFF'S CELL PHONE RINGS...") 68
BLESSING XXIII ("WHEN AUNT MILDRED FINISHED FALL LOVE...") 70
BLESSING XXIV ("THE REDWOOD TREES STAND...") 72
CURSE XVI ("MONEY'S A SORE SUBJECT FOR LYDIA...") 73
BLESSING XXV ("WHILE I WAS WRITING ROSALIND'S RING...") 76
BLESSING XXVI ("THE LOVERS WERE REUNITED AFTER 42 YEARS...") 77
CURSE XVII ("IN THE APARTMENT WE SHARED...") 79
BLESSING XXVII ("THE STUDENT LEADERS AT THE UNIVERSITY OF ALABAMA...") 81
CURSE XVIII ("IT'S SPRING AGAIN, LUCIE'S FAVORITE SEASON...") 83
BLESSING XXVIII ("POETS GIVE THEIR POEMS AWAY...") 84
CURSE XIX ("I LOST A SINGULAR FRIEND...") 85
BLESSING XXIX ("YEARS AGO I LIVED WITH A SECRET...") 88
CURSE XX ("ABBY RUNS ON A TREADMILL EVERY MORNING...") 89

BLESSING XXX ("THE RELIEF I FELT WHEN AT LAST...") 91
BLESSING XXXI ("I WRITE BETWEEN THE TICKING OF TWO CLOCKS...") 93
BLESSING XXXII ("AN ENCHANTED SUMMER EVENING...") 94
BLESSING XXXIII ("TWO GRASSES, TWISTED TOGETHER...") 95
CURSE XXI ("TO BE LEFT-HANDED IS TO BE...") 96
BLESSING XXXIV ("IN ONE DREAM I WAS TRAPPED...") 97
BLESSING XXXV ("SLOWLY I'M ACHIEVING...") 99
CURSE XXII ("ON SEPTEMBER 1, 1939...") 100
BLESSING XXXVI ("I WALKED OUT ON THE BEACH...") 103
BLESSING XXXVII ("ONCE A FRIEND INTERRUPTED ME...") 104
BLESSING XXXVIII ("IN SCIENCE, ELEGANCE...") 105
CURSE XXIII ("IN TWO MONTHS OF SIFTING THROUGH THE WRECKAGE..."). 106
BLESSING XXXIX ("SHAKING WITH FEVER...") 108
BLESSING XL ("ON THE FIRST DAY OF SPRING...") 109
CURSE XXIV ("OH, FOR THE POTENT SUBSTANCE...") 110
A BLESSING AND A CURSE ("ONE SUMMER AFTERNOON IN THE 1980S...") .. 112

END NOTES

AUTHOR BIO

End Notes

BLESSING VI: as reported by Corey Kilgannon, "Ax in Hand, A Hendrix Sings of Jimi's Legacy," *The New York Times*, 4/23/05.

BLESSING XXVI:
The quote at the end of the first stanza is from a letter from Seamus Heaney to Ted Hughes. The italicized lines are a quote from *That Morning* by Ted Hughes.

AUTHOR BIO

Anne Whitehouse was born and grew up in Birmingham, Alabama. She graduated from Harvard College and Columbia University. She is the author of *The Surveyor's Hand* (poems) and *Fall Love* (novel). Her second novel, *Rosalind's Ring,* set in Birmingham, is a finalist in the Santa Fe Writers Project Literary Awards. Her poetry chapbook, *Bear in Mind,* is forthcoming from Finishing Line Press. She lives in New York City with her husband and daughter. (www.annewhitehouse.com)

www.ingramcontent.com/pod-product-compliance
Lightning Source LLC
Chambersburg PA
CBHW070505100426
42743CB00010B/1766